I0447309

Love Passion Mandala Coloring

Copyright: Published in the United States by Kenny Tenney
Published December 2016
ISBN-13: 978-1541281486
ISBN-10: 1541281489

Thank you

www.ingramcontent.com/pod-product-compliance
Lightning Source LLC
Chambersburg PA
CBHW051946280526
45789CB00009B/3190
* 9 7 8 1 5 4 1 2 8 1 4 8 6 *